BATTLE
TANKS

IAN GRAHAM

© Aladdin Books Ltd 1990

Designed and produced by
Aladdin Books Ltd
28 Percy Street
London W1P 9FF

First published in
Great Britain in 1990 by
Gloucester Press
96 Leonard Street
London EC2A 4RH

ISBN 0-7496-0155-8

Design David West
Children's Book Design

Editorial Lionheart Books

Researcher Cecilia Weston-Baker

Illustrator Aziz Khan
Ron Hayward Associates

Printed in Belgium

CONTENTS

HOW · IT · WORKS

BATTLE
TANKS

IAN GRAHAM

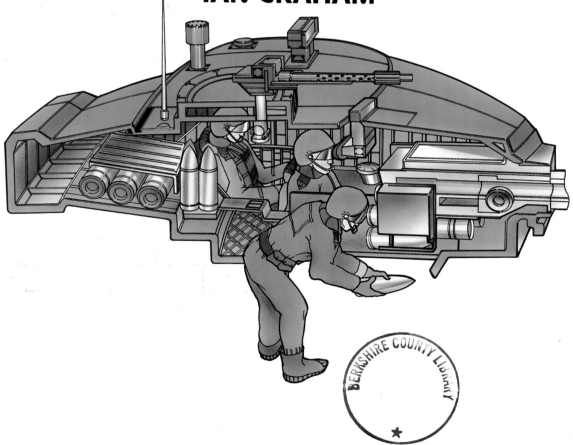

GLOUCESTER PRESS

London · New York · Toronto · Sydney

THE MAIN PARTS

The battle tank is the main weapon of modern land combat. Its job is to disable or destroy enemy tanks. Every tank is also therefore itself the target of another tank. It may also be attacked by a range of lethal weapons carried by soldiers and aircraft. To survive so that it can do the job it was designed for, it must be able to protect itself from these attacks.

The design of every tank is a combination of three important factors – mobility, protection and firepower. A powerful engine driving a pair of metal tracks gives it mobility. It is protected by a thick covering of heavy armour plate. Firepower may be provided by any of a variety of weapons, but by far the most important is the tank's main gun. This is mounted in a rotating compartment called a turret.

Some tanks are designed for very high speed and mobility. To save weight, they may carry less armour. Others are designed for maximum firepower and protection. The extra weight they have to carry reduces their mobility. This is why tanks come in many different shapes and sizes. Tank designers balance the three basic requirements in different ways.

The structure of the tank has two main components, the turret and the body, or hull. The hull must be large enough to hold the engine, fuel, weapon systems, ammunition and the tank's electronic systems, with enough space left over for the tank's crew of three or four.

A tank's electronic systems include fire control and radio communications. Fire control is a computerized system that helps the gunner to aim the main gun accurately. The tank may also be equipped with specialized instruments

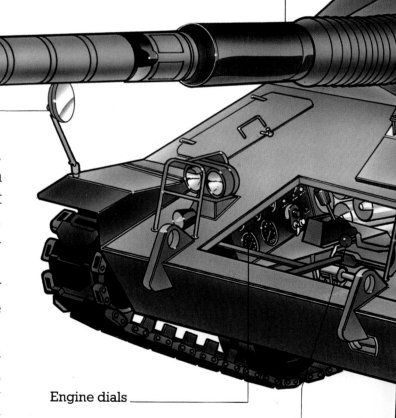

105mm low recoil gun

Wing mirror

Engine dials

Driver's controls

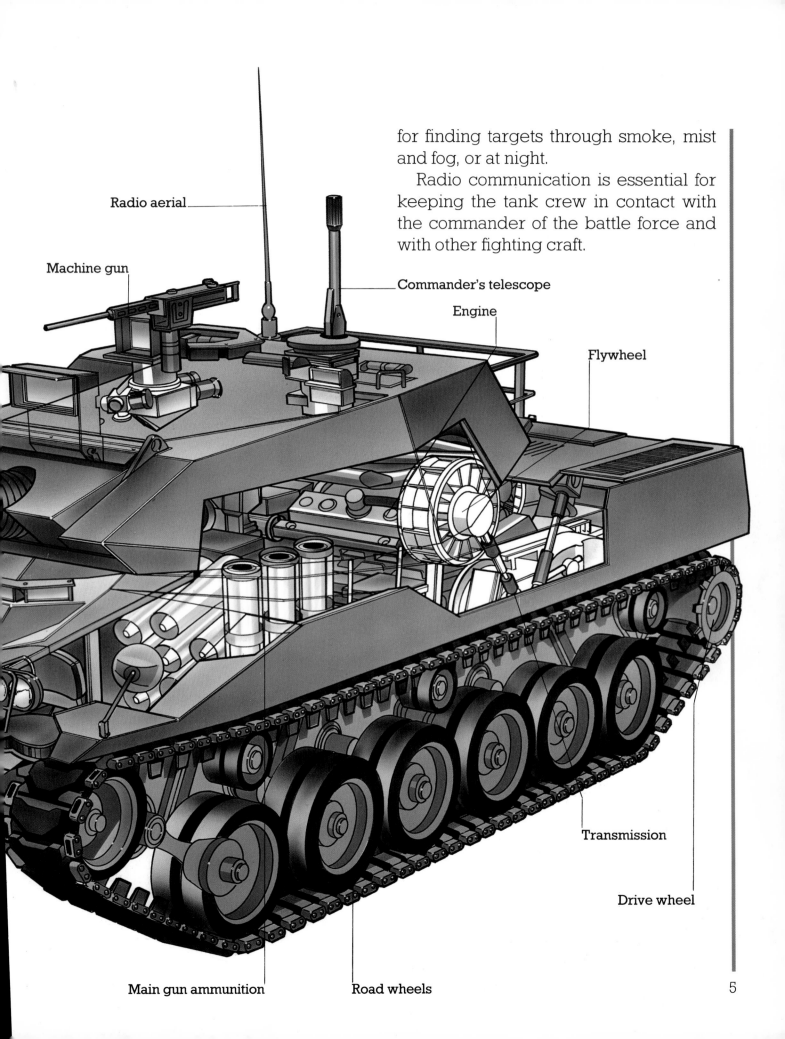

for finding targets through smoke, mist and fog, or at night.

Radio communication is essential for keeping the tank crew in contact with the commander of the battle force and with other fighting craft.

Radio aerial

Machine gun

Commander's telescope

Engine

Flywheel

Transmission

Drive wheel

Main gun ammunition

Road wheels

DIFFERENT TYPES

The main battle tank is only one of many different types of armoured combat vehicle. The battle tank is a very powerful general-purpose weapons system, but the others are designed to do more specialized jobs. They may use the same basic framework, or chassis, as the battle tank, but carry different weapons, tools or electronic systems.

Armoured personnel carriers equipped with lightweight guns transport small numbers of troops. Armoured engineering and recovery vehicles provide rescue and repair services for tanks. Missile carriers serve as mobile launching platforms. Lightweight tanks may be armed with a small main gun or a pair of anti-aircraft guns. Not all of these vehicles are tracked. Some of the smaller tanks have many wheels and no tracks.

One of the most specialized armoured vehicles is the bridge-layer. Bridges are often destroyed in war-time or there may not be a bridge where a commander wants to cross a river. The bridge-layer carries its own bridge, usually folded in half on top of the vehicle. At the river's edge, the bridge is unfolded across the water.

The British Challenger main battle tank.

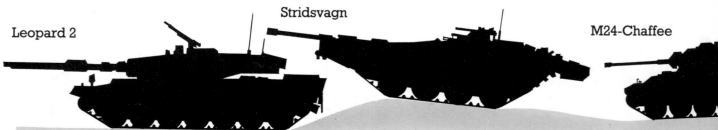

Leopard 2

Stridsvagn

M24-Chaffee

The M2 Bradley armoured personnel carrier.

The Swiss ADATS anti-aircraft tank.

The US M-60 bridge-laying tank.

The Swedish STRV-103 amphibious tank.

BTR-60   Chieftain   M110

ENGINES

A main battle tank can weigh over 50 tonnes. It needs an extremely powerful engine to move it along at speed. Most tanks are fitted with diesel engines. Some, like the German MTU engine that powers the Leopard 2 tank, are multi-fuel engines. They normally run on diesel oil, but they can be adjusted to use petrol or even jet fuel if diesel supplies are cut off.

A tank's performance depends on a combination of engine power and the weight of the tank. This is called the power-to-weight ratio. If two tanks are fitted with the same engine, but one tank is heavier than the other, the heavier tank will be the slower of the two. It will also use more fuel.

The only other type of engine used by tanks is the gas turbine. It is like an aircraft's jet engine, but in a tank its power is used to rotate a shaft that drives the tracks. The US M1 and Soviet T-80 main battle tanks are both gas turbine powered.

Almost all tanks have their engines fitted in a compartment at the back. This enables the crew, especially the driver, to work right at the front of the tank with a clear view ahead. Also, it means the front of the tank can be made low and sloping to deflect the blast from explosions. The turret and gun can be lower too, reducing the overall height of the tank. Even so, designers have experimented with front-mounted engines. The Israeli Merkava tank has the engine and transmission at the front. In this vehicle, a door in the rear of the hull allows three or four extra men to be carried, either infantrymen or casualties.

A diesel-engined tank speeding over land.

A tank's engine is changed.

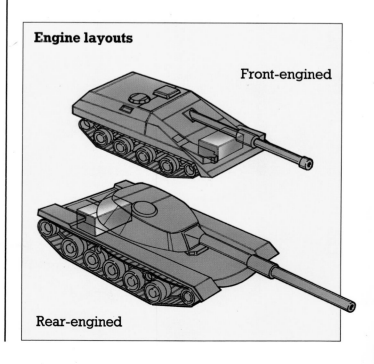

Engine layouts

Front-engined

Rear-engined

A tank's engine is linked to a pair of cog-wheels or sprockets through a system of gears called the transmission. The sprockets, one on each side of the tank at the rear, drive the tracks. This is also called the tank's powertrain.

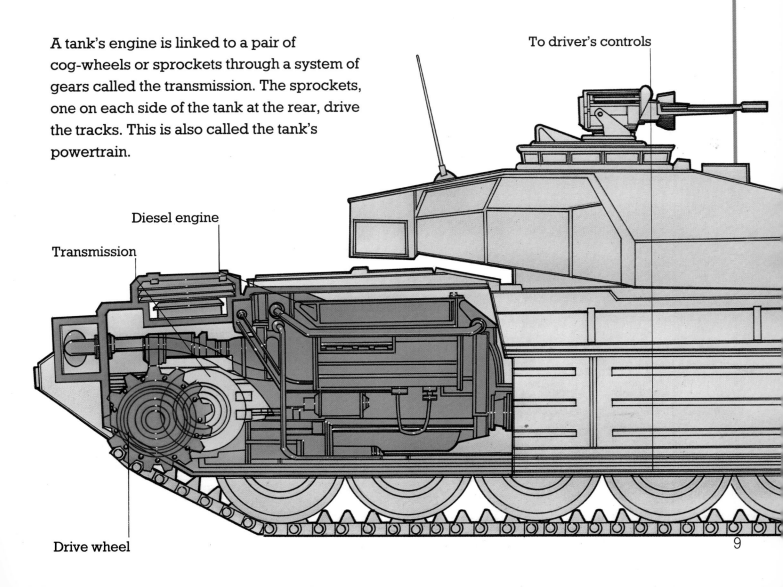

To driver's controls

Diesel engine

Transmission

Drive wheel

All main battle tanks have tracks.

The first successful suspension system developed for tanks was the Christie suspension (bottom right). It used large road wheels with solid rubber tyres. The wheels moved up and down against the action of springs or shock absorbers.

The next system to be developed was torsion bar suspension (top right). This is still the most commonly used system. Each road wheel is linked to a steel rod extending across the bottom of the hull. If the wheel moves up or down, the rod twists. It acts like a spring.

The most recently developed system is hydro-pneumatic suspension (centre right). This uses a cylinder of oil and gas as a spring. Vertical movements of the road wheels compress the gas in the cylinder and this has a "push-back" effect like the springiness in an air-cushion.

10

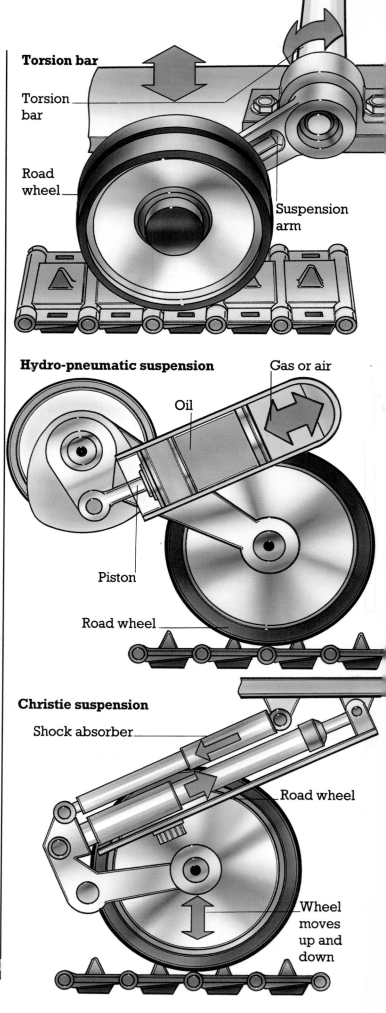

Torsion bar

Torsion bar

Road wheel

Suspension arm

Hydro-pneumatic suspension

Gas or air

Oil

Piston

Road wheel

Christie suspension

Shock absorber

Road wheel

Wheel moves up and down

TRACKS AND SUSPENSION

The most obvious difference between the main battle tank and most other military and civilian vehicles is that the tank's wheels are covered by flexible tracks. The tracks spread the great weight of the tank so that it does not sink into soft ground. They also help the tank to drive smoothly over bumps and holes in the ground. Tracks wear out and have to be replaced. The Leopard 2's tracks, for example, are replaced at least every 7,500km.

A tank's wheels are connected to the hull by springs and mechanical linkages called the suspension system. The suspension is very important because a tank's top speed is limited by the amount of hull vibration and bouncing the crew can tolerate.

There are several different types of suspension system but they all try to do the same thing. They allow the tank's wheels to move up and down, following the shape of the ground, while the hull remains quite steady. This enables the tank to travel faster over rough ground.

The height of a battle tank fitted with hydro-pneumatic suspension can be varied by pumping up the system's gas cylinders. The Swedish S-tank uses this in a unique way to raise and lower its gun. Pumping up the front suspension raises the gun (top). Pumping up the rear lowers the gun (above). The suspension can also lift the tank to "see" over obstacles or lower it to hide it.

When the tank is driving across level ground, the suspension system holds it almost perfectly horizontal.

When the tank comes to uneven ground, the road wheels move one by one while the hull and gun remain level.

Loading and firing

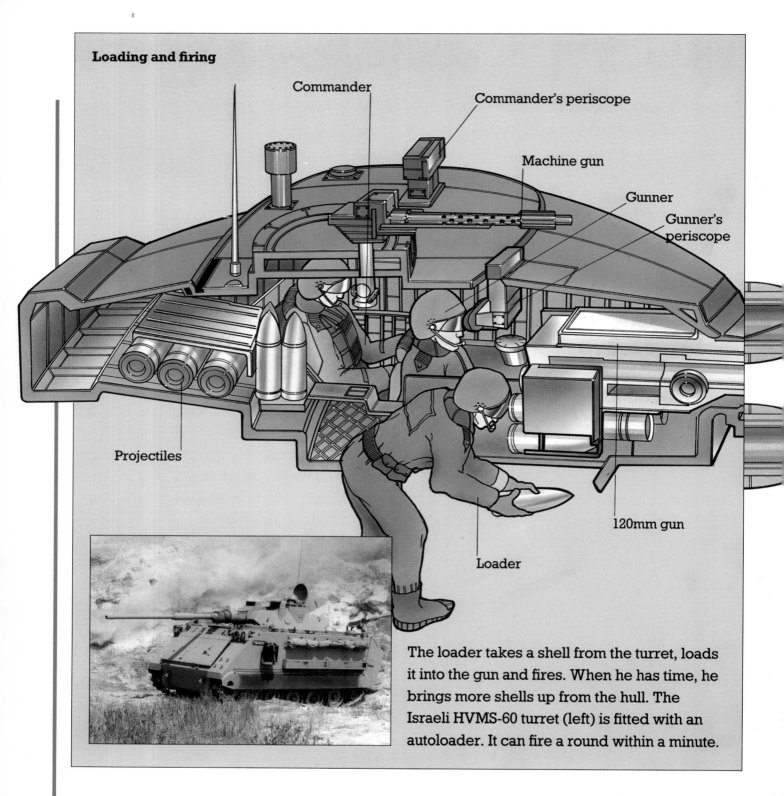

Commander

Commander's periscope

Machine gun

Gunner

Gunner's periscope

Projectiles

120mm gun

Loader

The loader takes a shell from the turret, loads it into the gun and fires. When he has time, he brings more shells up from the hull. The Israeli HVMS-60 turret (left) is fitted with an autoloader. It can fire a round within a minute.

The main gun can be raised (middle right) and lowered (far right). When the tank is moving, it is normally carried level (right) as this is the most stable position. The safest firing position is "hull down" with the tank on one side of a ridge, firing down on the target (far right) beyond the ridge. This exposes the least turret and hull area to an enemy.

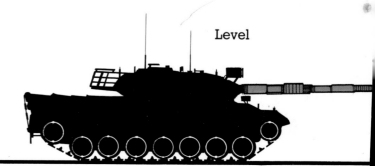

Level

TURRETS AND GUNS

Most tank guns have a rifled barrel (below). Its spiral grooves make the shell spin as it is projected forward and keep it pointing at the target as it flies through the air.

Some guns have a smooth-bore barrel (bottom) for firing armour-piercing projectiles which are stabilized by fins instead of spinning.

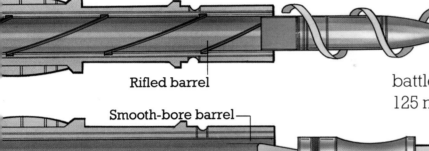

Rifled barrel

Smooth-bore barrel

A battle tank in action.

The turret is the tank's fighting compartment. It carries the main gun and it is motorized so that it can be rotated quickly. The gun is aimed by rotating the turret and tilting the barrel up, which is called elevation, or down, called depression. The turret's shape and height limit how much the gun can be depressed. Its size is measured by the width of the hole through the barrel, known as its calibre. Main battle tanks are fitted with guns of 105 to 125 millimetres calibre.

The barrel is made as long as possible because this makes the gun more accurate. If it is too long, it can bend or vibrate due to its weight. Temperature differences along its length resulting from the firing of shells can also cause bending. This can be solved by covering the barrel with a sleeve to spread the heat more evenly. Vibration and bending can also be reduced by making the barrel stiffer. Some tanks are fitted with a system that detects barrel droop and corrects for it when aiming. In addition to the main gun, the turret may carry several machine guns mounted on top of the turret.

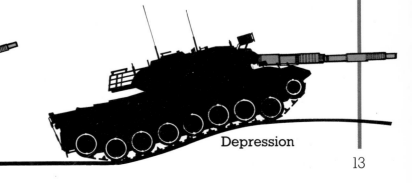

Elevation

Depression

A battle tank hit on the turret.

Until the end of World War II, tank guns were made increasingly large to fire larger shells. The invention of sub-calibre ammunition ended this trend. These shells are made long and thin to minimize air resistance. This ensures that they hit the target at the maximum speed. They must also be very hard to punch their way through tank armour. They are usually made from tungsten metal. Conventional shells are kept pointing at the target, or stabilized, while they are in flight by making them spin. Spin stabilization does not work with long, thin ammunition. Instead, they are stabilized by a set of tail fins. But all shells wobble slightly on leaving a gun before they fly through the air straight. As they reach the limit of the gun's range, they wobble again.

The Armour-Piercing Fin Stabilized Discarding Sabot round has three parts. The long, thin penetrator (1) is encased in a collar called a sabot (2). In flight, it is stabilized by tail fins (3).

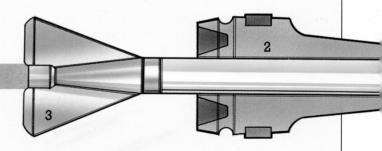

A High Explosive Squash Head (HESH) round is composed of a propellant (4), a fuse (5) and a charge of high explosives (6). The nose of the round is deliberately made soft to collapse on impact and detonate the explosives against the hull.

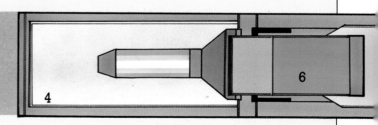

The warhead of a High Explosive Anti-Tank (HEAT) round (7) is specially shaped to concentrate its blast in a small area. In flight, like the APFSDS round, HEAT is stabilized by tail fins (8).

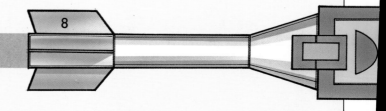

AMMUNITION

Three main types of armour-attack ammunition are in current use – High Explosive Anti-Tank (HEAT), High Explosive Squash Head (HESH) and sub-calibre. They work in different ways. A HEAT round is detonated at a precise distance from the target's armour. A cone-shaped hollow in front of the explosives focuses the energy of the explosion on to a tiny spot, blasting a hole through the armour. HEAT is also called hollow-charge ammunition. A HESH round contains explosives packed inside a soft case. When it hits a tank, the case collapses and the explosives squash against the armour. When it explodes, pieces of metal called scabs are blown off the armour inside the tank.

Sub-calibre ammunition uses a thin, sharp dart of very hard metal to punch a hole through armour. It is much thinner than the gun-barrel calibre, hence the name sub-calibre. To make it a tight fit inside the barrel, it is surrounded by a collar called a sabot, which drops away in flight. Sub-calibre ammunition is also called Armour Piercing Discarding Sabot ammunition (APDS) or APFSDS if it uses fin stabilization (FS).

An anti-tank missile hits its target with devastating effect.

HITTING THE TARGET

If a tank's gun were pointed directly at a target and fired, the round would hit the ground before it reached the target. As the round flies through the air, it is pulled down by gravity. The gun must therefore be aimed higher than the target, at an angle called the elevation angle. It depends on the distance between tank and target, the range. As the range increases, so must the elevation.

The first tank gunners had to guess the range. As guns became more powerful and ranges increased, guess-

work became quite useless. Optical rangefinders were developed, but were unpopular with many gunners, who preferred to use a ranging machine gun (RMG) mounted beside the main gun. Firing this gave the target's range and the main gun could then be set accurately. The most modern tanks use laser rangefinders. A laser beam is fired at the target. The time taken for the reflected beam to return is used by a computer to calculate the range and set the main gun.

A tank crew locates a target moving from left to right. The gunner triggers his laser rangefinder.

The moving target option is selected and a grid appears in the gun sight. It is set to match the target speed.

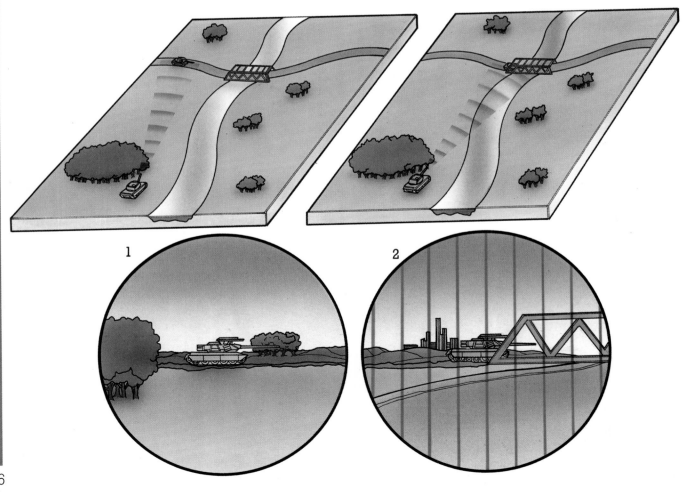

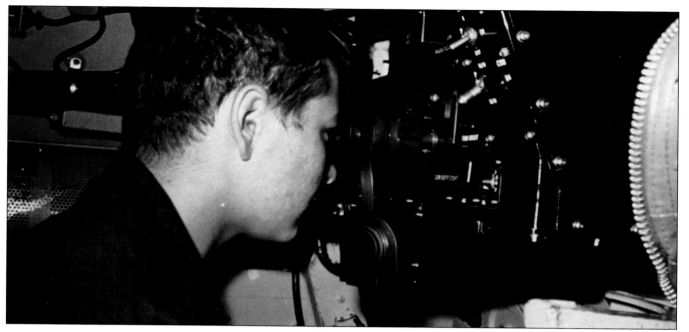

A tank commander and gunner seated at their sights.

A computer calculates the range, speed and direction of the target and displays an aiming mark.

If the gunner now aims at this position and fires, the round should score a direct hit on the target.

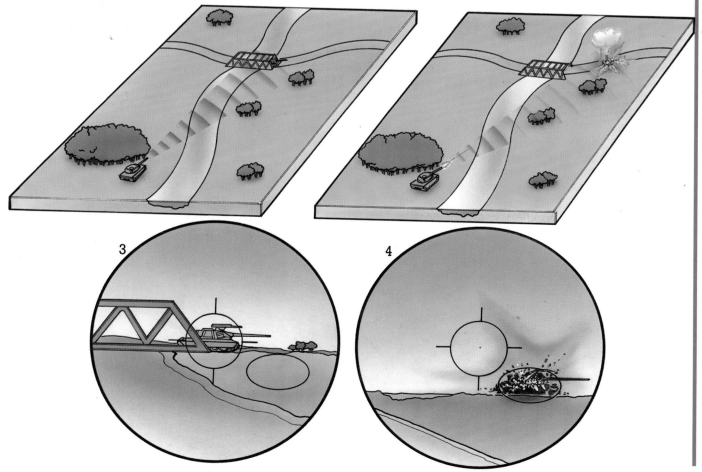

A tank crew has to work in very cramped and noisy conditions.

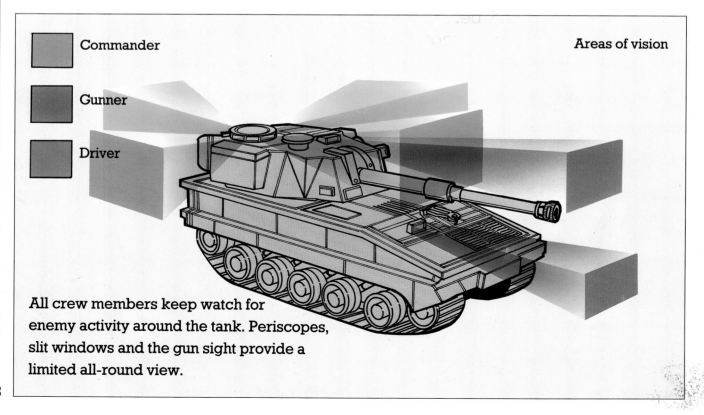

Commander

Gunner

Driver

Areas of vision

All crew members keep watch for enemy activity around the tank. Periscopes, slit windows and the gun sight provide a limited all-round view.

THE CREW

Most modern tanks are designed to carry a crew of four – commander, loader, gunner and driver. Until World War II, a bow (front) gunner was also carried. As battle ranges increased, the bow gunner became unnecessary. The loader can be replaced by an automatic loading system, or autoloader, enabling the tank to operate with a crew of only three. The Swedish S-tank was the first to use an autoloader.

Each crew member has a particular job to do, but some jobs are shared. The commander decides what the tank will do, acting on orders from battle-control received by radio. The gunner operates the gunsight, rangefinder, fire control system and, of course, the main gun itself. The loader ensures that the main gun is always loaded and ready to fire. The driver controls the tank's engine and movements. All crew members use their various sights and periscopes to look for the enemy and report any sightings to the commander.

Most tanks are rear-engined and have a four-man crew, but there are other arrangements. The driver of a three- or four-man rear-engined tank sits at the front in the middle. If the tank is front-engined, the driver sits to one side, beside the engine. In a three-man front-engined tank, the driver can be moved back into the turret, allowing the height of the tank to be reduced. This makes the vehicle a smaller target to enemy tanks. The arrangement is based on the Soviet T-72. The tank's height could also be reduced if the driver worked lying face down, but this is still experimental.

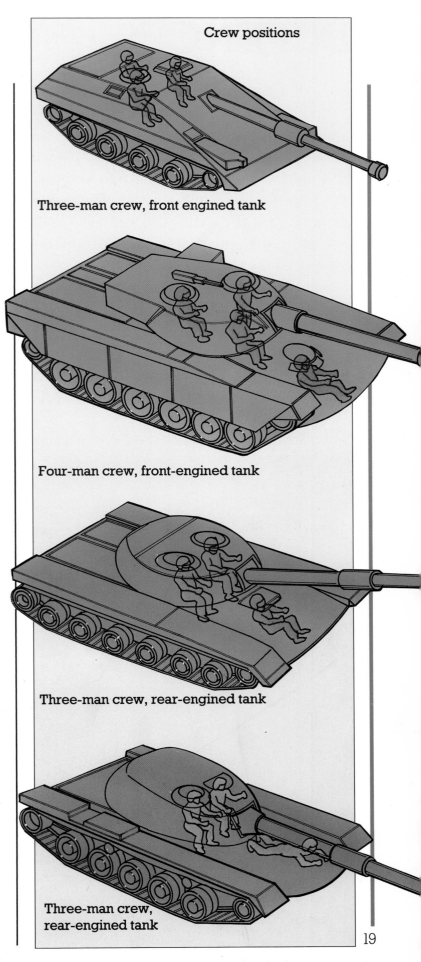

Crew positions

Three-man crew, front engined tank

Four-man crew, front-engined tank

Three-man crew, rear-engined tank

Three-man crew, rear-engined tank

DEFENCES

As each new type of weapon or ammunition is developed for attacking tanks, a new means of defence must also be developed. The tank's armour is an effective defence against all but the most specialized anti-armour weapons. Armour-piercing shot is most effective against vertical surfaces. It can be deflected by sloping the armour.

Sloping armour also presents a greater thickness to the shot, making it more difficult for armour-piercing shot to get through.

New types of armour have been developed to defeat anti-tank weapons by deflecting the shot or absorbing its energy. Chobham armour, named after the British research establishment where it was developed, is secret, but it is believed to be a sandwich of metal and plastic sheets.

The latest development is known as active or reactive armour. The tank is covered by panels that are designed to explode when struck. When any shot hits one of these panels, it explodes outwards against the shot. Israeli tanks were the first to use active armour, which they call Blazer armour. Soviet tanks are now using it too.

Camouflage paint and netting breaks up a tank's outline and makes it more difficult to see.

Laminated armour is an effective defence against anti-tank shot. It is made from a sandwich of different materials. Most of the shot's energy is absorbed by the outer armour and a soft metal or plastic layer underneath. Rods of titanium metal between the plates are designed to deflect armour-piercing rounds. Sloping the armour also helps by increasing its horizontal thickness. Sometimes, sheets of steel are added to a tank's original armour plating to give it more protection. This outer layer absorbs much of a shell's energy.

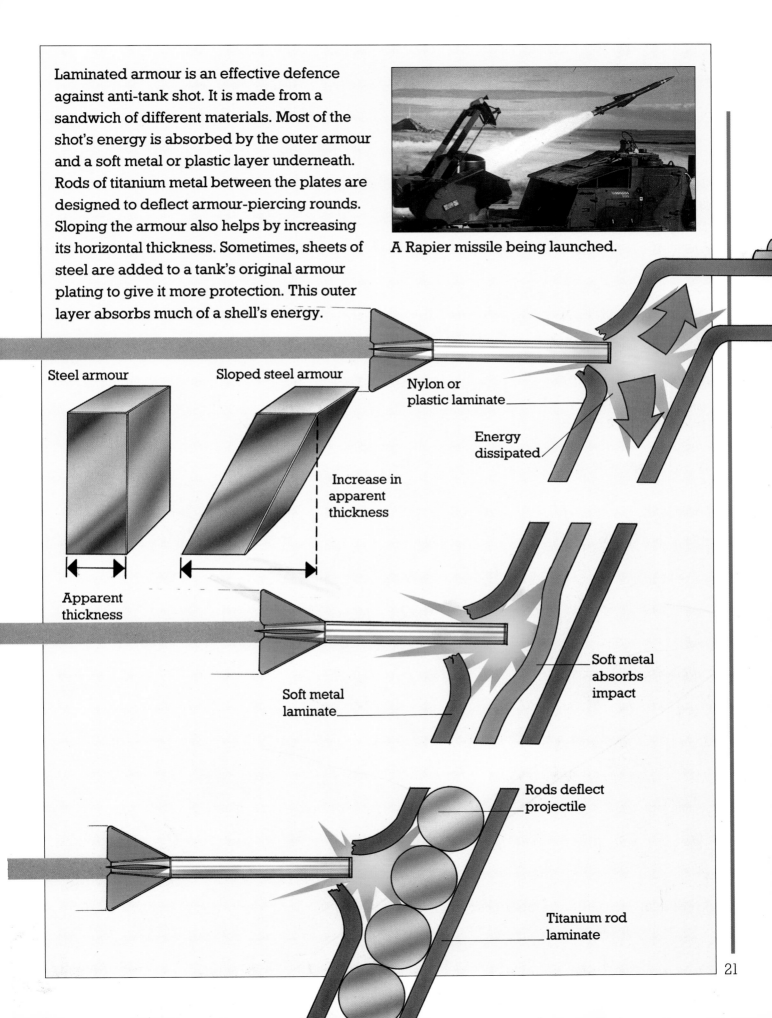

A Rapier missile being launched.

Steel armour

Sloped steel armour

Increase in apparent thickness

Apparent thickness

Nylon or plastic laminate

Energy dissipated

Soft metal laminate

Soft metal absorbs impact

Rods deflect projectile

Titanium rod laminate

IN COMBAT

All armies study combat so that they can plan how to use their forces. The Soviet, US and British armies agree on the importance of surprising the enemy with a powerful attack force, but they differ in other respects.

The Soviet Union stresses the great importance of a swift attack. Soviet tank commanders are expected to advance by at least 30km per day. The US Army emphasizes intelligence gathering, the collection of all sorts of information about the battlefield, and also the destruction of enemy defences. The British Army uses its tanks in a more flexible way than the others, adapting swiftly to the changing events on the battlefield.

Tanks are never used alone. They are always part of a larger combined force. This might include aeroplanes, helicopters, a variety of armoured vehicles, artillery (heavy guns) and infantry troops. The combined force's attack is led by tanks. They try to destroy other tanks and artillery positions to prepare the way for the rest of the force. They can also smash their way through thick woods, fences and even buildings to open up pathways for the troops following behind them.

A combined force attacks. Light tanks (1) advance and observe the enemy. They report back to the main battle tanks (2). Aircraft support the land force.

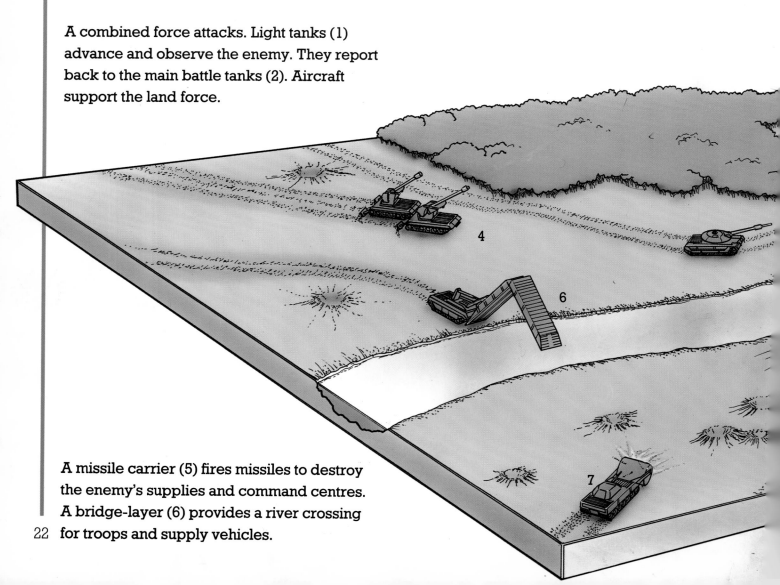

A missile carrier (5) fires missiles to destroy the enemy's supplies and command centres. A bridge-layer (6) provides a river crossing for troops and supply vehicles.

This tank has found a safe firing position and selected its target.

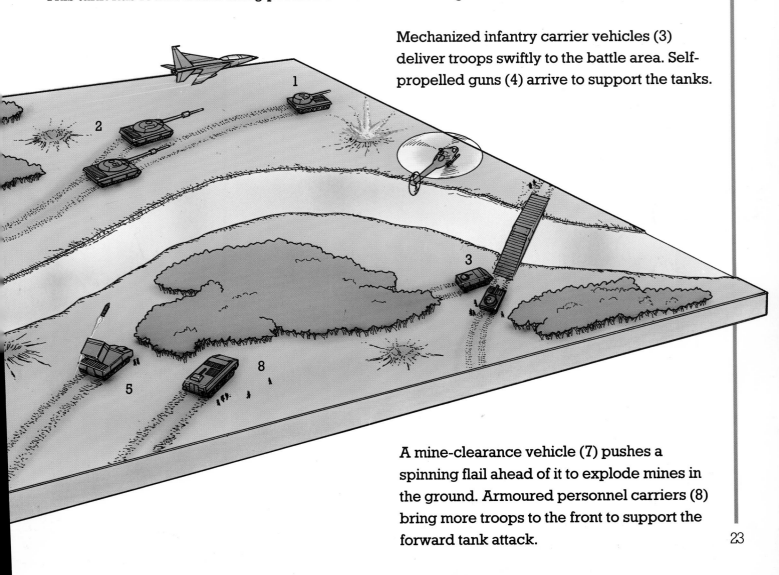

Mechanized infantry carrier vehicles (3) deliver troops swiftly to the battle area. Self-propelled guns (4) arrive to support the tanks.

A mine-clearance vehicle (7) pushes a spinning flail ahead of it to explode mines in the ground. Armoured personnel carriers (8) bring more troops to the front to support the forward tank attack.

ANTI-TANK WEAPONS

During a ground attack, it is vital to destroy enemy tanks before they can dominate the battlefield. Infantry soldiers can now attack armoured vehicles using a range of anti-tank weapons. They are light enough to be carried by one or two soldiers and also powerful enough to stop a main battle tank. They are also called recoilless weapons. Recoil is a force that acts in the opposite direction to a shell or missile when it is fired, making the gun jump backwards.

Large guns must be fixed securely to heavy bases with dampers to absorb the recoil. To make a weapon sufficiently lightweight for soldiers to use without a heavy base, the recoil is eliminated by using a barrel that is open at both the back and the front.

The anti-tank guided missile is by far the most effective portable anti-tank weapon in use now. It is a rocket with a HEAT warhead. When the missile is fired, it remains connected to the launcher by a long wire. The operator keeps the target in the middle of his sight. Control signals sent along the wire guide the missile on to the target.

The European Milan and the US TOW (Tube-launched, Optically-tracked Wire guided) are good examples of anti-tank guided weapons (ATGW).

The Dragon anti-tank missile system is designed for one-man operation. The launcher weighs only 14kg – about the same as a bicycle – and the missile another 6kg. Its 2.45kg charge of high explosives can blast through up to 60cm of armour plate at a range of up to 1,100m.

A helicopter homes in on its tank target and fires an anti-tank missile.

Dragon shoulder-fired anti-tank missile.

An infantryman attacks a tank.

The most serious threat to tanks now comes from armed helicopters such as the American Cobra. These carry missiles and fast-firing cannons, which can be aimed at a tank and kept on target while the helicopter is maneouvring in the air. Helicopters cannot be heard easily by the tank crew and they can attack at very high speeds from any direction. Among the most widely used anti-tank missiles is the British Swingfire. Its flightpath can be changed dramatically after launch by means of a jetavator. This is a swivelling nozzle at the rear through which the propulsion jet passes. The flight control and sighting unit can be separated from the launcher, which can be positioned out of sight. Swingfire's range is 4,000 metres.

Damage to tank's underside which has no armour.

THE FUTURE

Tank design is continually changing as engineers experiment with new materials, systems and ways of using tanks. The Israeli Merkava tank, already in production, has many new features. With the engine at the front, it can have rear doors for crew escape and loading ammunition. Its turret is specially shaped to present a small target to the enemy. Future tanks may not have turrets. In the "gun-over-hull" design the gun is fixed to the top of the hull and operated remotely by the crew in the armoured hull below.

Tanks need tracks to spread their weight over a large area, but tracks also limit a tank's manoeuvrability. The Swedish UDES XX-20 bends in the middle to combine a long track length with greatly improved manoeuvrability. Remotely controlled robot tanks are also being developed. They would be used to clear minefields and observe enemy positions by day or night using video cameras and night vision systems.

Future tanks will be faster and more manoeuvrable. They will not rely on armour alone for protection. The Israeli Merkava tank already has an explosion and fire protection and suppression system. It extinguishes any fire in the crew compartment in a fraction of a second. The Swedish UDES XX-20 attempts to make a tank more agile by splitting it in two. US engineers have built an agile tank test vehicle to study the benefits of greater mobility. Another idea is to design a basic hull to which any one of various "pods" can be fitted – gun turret pod, crane pod and so on.

The US HIMAG experimental tank is tested.

The US HSTV.

The Israeli Merkava main battle tank incorporates many novel features.

HISTORY OF TANKS

The tank was developed during World War I. It was the result of the need for a new type of vehicle to cope with conditions on the battlefields. In 1916, the Mark 1 Tank was the first tank to enter service. The 28-tonne British tank carried its four-man crew at a top speed of only 6.4kph. At this time, tanks were also being developed in France. The first, the St Chamond, went into action in 1917. It used a farm tractor's tracks.

The first tank, the British Mark I – "Mother".

Germany was slow to recognize the value of the tank and begin building its own. The German A7V was not built until the war was almost over.

The United States joined World War I in 1917 and US engineers began designing tanks. US inventor J Walter Christie introduced new ideas that were copied in later Soviet and British tanks. The Christie suspension system was very successful. It enabled Christie's M1919 tank to drive on wheels or tracks. The Christie M1928 had a top speed of 112kph on wheels and 67kph on tracks. The landing craft that took soldiers from ships on to beaches in World War II were like Christie amphibious vehicles.

The Christie M1931 tank.

After World War I, the major military powers set about developing more advanced tanks. The Soviet Union was particularly keen to develop very large armoured units of heavy tanks. Germany favoured lighter, faster tanks.

The standard German light tank was the Panzer Kampfwagen IID. Germany also developed new ways of using tanks. Britain and France used their tanks in groups and formations like fleets of ships. Their tanks were also often split up into small attack groups. German tanks were used in concentrated, unstoppable attacks. When they seized ground, they left its defence to artillery guns, freeing the tanks to attack elsewhere. This proved to be very successful.

A WWII German Panzer Kampfwagen.

The German Panther D was one of the most successful tanks of World War II. It was designed to combat the Soviet T34. The most successful US tank of the war was the Medium M4 Sherman.

The British Centurion tank of the 1940s-1960s.

British tank design lagged behind other nations until the Centurion Mark 1 was developed in 1945, just too late for war service. The Centurion Mark 3 had an electronically stabilized gun. The Centurion remained in service with the British Army until the 1960s.

The US M1 Abrams battle tank of the 1980s.

Centurion was replaced by Chieftain, which has now been replaced by Challenger. The Soviet Union's latest tank is the T-80, the first Soviet tank to have a gas turbine engine.

Facts and Figures

The first tank ever built was the British experimental No.1 Lincoln, which became known as Little Willie. It ran for the first time in September 1915.

Tanks were used in battle for the first time at the battle of Fleurs-Courcelette in France in September 1916.

The first battle between tanks took place at the French village of Villers Bretonneux during World War I. On 24 April 1918, 14 German A7V tanks fought with three British Mark IV and seven Whippet tanks. The German tanks came out of the encounter best.

The heaviest tank ever built was the German Panzer Kampfwagen Maus II. It weighed over 190 tonnes. It was designed for use in World War II, but when production models were not ready by the time the war ended, the project was abandoned.

The heaviest tank to enter service was the French Char de Rupture 2C bis. Built in 1922, it weighed over 75 tonnes and needed a crew of 13.

The fastest tank in the world is the British Scorpion lightweight tank. The Scorpion can reach a speed of over 80kph. To save weight, its hull is made from welded aluminium instead of steel plate. It is also amphibious.

GLOSSARY

blitzkrieg
From the German words meaning a lightning war. A powerful, swift attack intended to defeat the enemy quickly.

breech
The part of a gun, behind the barrel, where the ammunition is loaded.

calibre
The internal diameter of a gun barrel and the diameter of the round or shot that the weapon fires.

elevation
The angle through which a gun is raised or lowered to aim at a target.

laser
A device used to produce an intense, perfectly straight and narrow, beam of light, used in laser rangefinders, laser gyroscopes and target markers.

link
One of the metal parts that make up a tank's tracks.

machine gun
A gun capable of rapid, automatic fire.

MBT
Main Battle Tank, now the largest type.

MICV
Mechanized Infantry Combat Vehicle. An armoured troop carrier with its own armament. Alternatively known as an Armoured Fighting Vehicle (AFV).

muzzle
The end of a barrel where a shell or missile emerges when fired; it is the opposite end to the breech.

ordnance
Ammunition and explosives.

projectile
An object fired from a gun – a bullet, shell, shot or missile.

RADAR
RAdio Detection And Ranging. A system invented in the 1940s for locating objects by bouncing radio waves off them and analysing the echoes.

rifling
The spiral grooves cut into a gun barrel to make a bullet or shell spin when it is fired, to stabilize it.

ROBAT
Robotic Obstacle Breaching Tank. A remotely controlled tank designed for observation and mine detection.

round
A single bullet, projectile or projectile plus its propellant charge.

sabot
A collar fitted around sub-calibre shot to make it fit a barrel.

secondary armament
Weapons such as machine guns fitted to a tank in addition to its main gun.

self-propelled gun
A gun mounted on a motorized carrier such as a tank or aircraft.

shell
A hollow projectile filled with high explosives.

shot
A solid projectile most usually used for piercing armour.

sub-calibre
Shot that is much slimmer than the calibre of a barrel, fired inside a sabot which falls away in flight.

tracer
Ammunition that can be seen after firing because of a burning material at the base of the projectile. Tracers can be used to set the elevation of a larger gun.

tracks
The flexible metal belts that cover a tank's road wheels. They may be made entirely of metal links or partly of metal and partly of rubber. They provide a means of movement and steering.

trajectory
The curving path of a projectile after it is fired from a gun.

warhead
The nose of a missile or shell that contains the explosives.

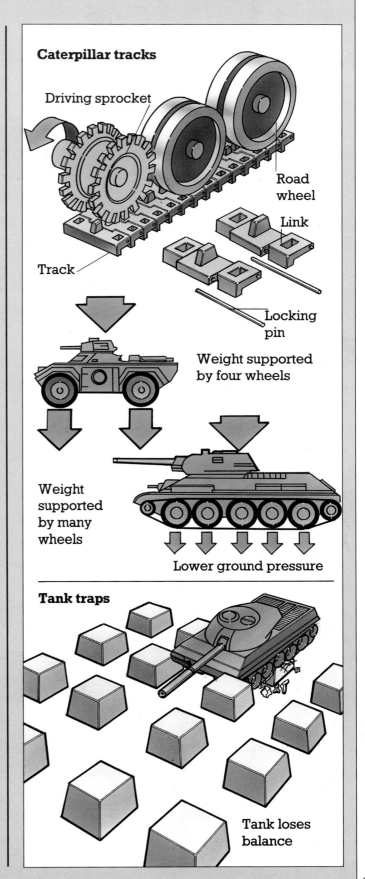

Caterpillar tracks

Driving sprocket

Road wheel

Link

Track

Locking pin

Weight supported by four wheels

Weight supported by many wheels

Lower ground pressure

Tank traps

Tank loses balance

INDEX

Photographic credits
Cover: William Fowler; pages 6, 7 all, 8, 9, 10, 12, 13, 14, 15, 17, 20, 23, 24, 25, 26, 30 both and 31 both: Military Archive Research Services; pages 7 and 27: Salamander; page 11: Swedish Defence Force; pages 18, 21 and 27: Topham Picture Library.